My family and I reviewed this book and are
ten, published and available. This is an ideal
my husband and I are), parents (which my
disabilities (which my nephew is). We think ... .
hands of educators, parents and students. This story is exhilarating
and sad but teaches us important information about the journey that
so many folks with disabilities take. Thank you for your contribution,
and I am hopeful and optimistic that it will get great visibility and
distribution.

Mary A. Falvey, Ph.D.
Dean, Charter College of Education
California State University, Los Angeles

I have had the pleasure of reviewing the Eileen Kushner story and
found it both moving and motivating. This is a story I would recommend for readers of all ages who understand the importance of hard
work and commitment regardless of disabilities or other drawbacks.
Eileen's story tells us all that with hard work, success is attainable.
I highly recommend this book for students who have special needs,
for parents who have special needs children and for teachers and staff
who work with our special needs students. There are numerous lessons
on how each of us affect the lives of children, how important it is to
see each child as a capable and contributing human being and to understand that our special needs students have a great deal to contrib-
ute to society. Eileen Kushner's story is the story of hope. It is the story
of a beautiful family and mentors who supported Eileen to the high
levels of success that she has reached today. Most important, Eileen's
story is that of giving back and supporting others so that they may
see themselves as contributing citizens regardless of their disability.
I encourage everyone to spend a few minutes and become a part of
this great American story.

Alice Petrossian
President, Association of California School Administrators

I was deeply touched emotionally while reading *Smart on the Inside,* a true story describing Eileen Kushner's painful yet successful journey in life. This beautifully written book is a must read for people struggling with learning disabilities, or anyone who has faced adversity. It will give them hope, even through the dark times. Eileen's strong message of working hard, seeking help and having a positive attitude can also change others' lives.

Sharyl Kennedy
Executive Director of Horizon Academy
Specializing in Educating Students with Learning Disabilities

Having worked in the field of special education for many years, I have had the opportunity to read and hear many stories of how people with disabilities have faced and overcome challenges presented by the world. Eileen's story stands out to me in its simplicity and the straightforward manner Kathy Young uses to tell that compelling story.

I believe that Eileen's experiences and feelings, as described in *Smart on the Inside,* will resonate with anyone who feels "different" and especially with students with disabilities at the upper elementary to secondary grade level. I also believe that the McDonald's Corporation sends a loud message about the benefits that can come to corporate America when they put aside a "one size fits all" method of assessing a job applicant's abilities.

Ms. Young did an excellent job of portraying Eileen's ordeal in a natural, credible style and avoiding the inclination to over-dramatize events and emotions that are often present in stories about overcoming disabilities. Eileen is so brave and generous to share her life with those who can benefit from her story. She is clearly a remarkable person on many levels.

Joseph Green
Specialist, Transition
Los Angeles Unified School District (LAUSD)

A True Story About Succeeding
in Spite of Learning Disabilities

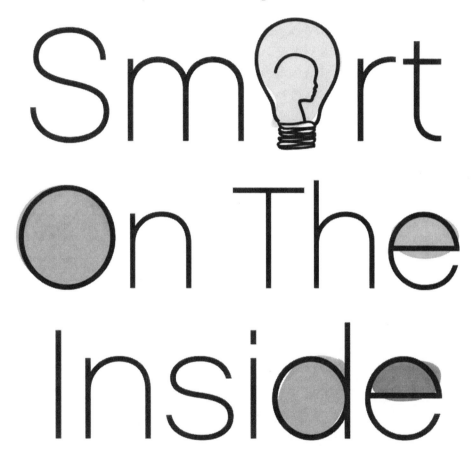

Smart On The Inside

Eileen Gold Kushner As Told By Kathy Young

Eileen Gold Kushner

Writers of the Round Table Press
PO Box 511
Highland Park, IL 60035

Writers of the Round Table Press name and logo are trademarks of Round Table Companies and Writers of the Round Table Inc.

Cover design by Analee Paz
Interior design and layout by Sunny DiMartino

Printed in the United States of America

First Edition: July 2012
10 9 8 7 6 5 4 3 2 1

Library of Congress Cataloging-in-Publication Data

Kushner, Eileen Gold; Young, Kathy.
Smart on the Inside: The True Story About Succeeding in Spite of Learning Disabilities /
Eileen Gold Kushner, Kathy Young.—1st ed. p. cm.
ISBN: 9781610660556
Library of Congress Control Number: 2012942045

Smart On The Inside

Eileen and Larry on their 50th Anniversary

Dedication

by Eileen Gold Kushner

NEVER in my wildest wildest dreams would I have imagined that I would know so many wonderful people who have changed my life and given me back some of the self-confidence that I lost during my school years. Being told at the age of 11 that I would *NEVER* amount to anything because I could not read, spell or do math like the other kids in my classes set me up to feel like a failure for years and years. These people all played a part in my success.

First, I want to thank my wonderful husband, **Larry Kushner**, who not once in all the years that I've known him (over 50) ever laughed at or belittled my skills. He has helped me learn so many things, including how to count money, read, write letters and send e-mails. Thank you for always stopping whatever you were doing and in your most calm voice helping me figure out how to solve a problem, spell a word, or look up information in a book. You never lost your patience with me. Now that's *LOVE*!

Since I was told that I might never have children, I consider my girls to be my gifts. We have three wonderful daughters, **Laura, Debbie,** and **Elyse**. I helped them learn to read, write and spell even though I did not have the skills to teach them the conventional way. I always helped them complete their homework using my own learning strategies and it *worked*! I helped educate them so that they were able to earn Master's degrees and become a Teacher/Principal, Speech Pathologist, and a Physical Therapist. They have also become the best moms in the world.

I would also like to thank my "munchkins," our seven grandchildren: **Hannah, Danny, Alison, Noah, Carly, Lindsey,** and **Natalie,** who have taught me what really is important in life.

To my parents, **Dave** and **Etta Gold,** who died much too young in life and never knew what I have achieved in my life, thank you, **Mom** and **Dad,** for all that you gave me and did for me. Our family did not have much money, but we were rich with love.

To my brother, **Stephen Gold,** thank you for everything you had to put up with being the older brother to a set of twins.

To my twin brother, **Elliot Gold,** I would like to thank you for being my protector.

To my sister-in-law, **Shirley Gold,** thank you for choosing the wonderful title, *Smart on the Inside.*

To my friend, **Carol Goldberg,** thank you for encouraging me to share my story.

Thank you to my FRIEND and my TEACHER, **Kathy Young.** I don't know where to start to thank you for all the energy you put into our story, and it is *OUR* story. If you had not come into my life when you did, I would not have been able to get the word out to so many people. *OUR* book is all about people believing in themselves. With your gentle guidance, look what we have accomplished! Thank you so much for working with me to educate kids, teachers and parents. I never knew it was going to take so much of my personal energy to tell you my story so you could put it on paper. You listened to me cry, laugh and remember things that sometimes I didn't want to remember. You rewrote and rewrote and rewrote lines, words and paragraphs and never blinked an eye. You were *ALWAYS* by my side just to listen and never make judgements. You were just wonderful as I sat and cried to you as I tried to remember all the experiences that made me what I am today. You truly are my friend, business partner, and sister. And, after five long years of working together, we have finished OUR book, and I can never thank you enough.

—*Eileen Gold Kushner*

Dedication

by Kathy Young

This book is dedicated to Jason, Maddy, Mari, Danny, Brad, Tracy, Megan, Eric, Michelle, Jennifer, Ariel, Rachel, Adam, Jamie, Stefanie, Ellen, Ashley, Kevin, Shana, Samantha, Sarah, Zach, Jessica, Kenny, Caitlin, Brian, Alyssa, Matt, Alex, Tony, Alan, Gail, Joel, Kevin, A. J., Derek, Aaron, Jacob,Steven, Leah, Ashlee, Nathan and <u>all</u> my students who taught me so much about learning.

Thank you to the successful adults with learning disabilities who came to school to speak to my students about succeeding in spite of learning disabilities: **P. Buckley Moss (Artist), Caroline Janover (Author), Sharyl Kennedy (Executive Director), Andy (Businessman), Doug (Superintendent), Jason (Actor), Carrie (Teacher), Mike (Social Worker), Howard (Doctor), Roger (Artist), Nicole (Teacher), Dee (Radio Talk Show Host), Jim (Carpenter), Beth (Journalist) Jody (Eye Doctor), Dara (Lawyer).**

Thank you to Jan Benkoske for working with me on all the bulletin boards for Eileen's McDonald's restaurants. Each year, I would tell you the theme, and you were able to figure out how my students could create an artistic, educational display that was seen by thousands of customers.

Thank you to Jackie Neumann, who helped us with those bulletin boards for a few years. Since my retirement she and her students have continued to help us create educational displays.

Thank you to Marcia Tillett-Zinzow, whose excellent suggestions years ago helped me turn a short story into a book.

Thank you to Stacy Lipshutz for editing the original versions of this book.

Thank you to the teachers, special education teachers and aides, who worked with me to help students succeed in spite of their learning differences.

Thank you to Marianne and Kathy, who always helped me and encouraged my students with the Service Learning Projects.

Thank you to Larry B. for donating so many items to our fund-raising efforts.

Thank you to my mom, Barbara, for participating in the fund-raising activities, Learning Disabilities Simulation, Lambda Delta events, and field trips. Thank you for baking your delicious chocolate chip cookies.

Thank you to my parents, Bob and Barbara Bock, who taught me the value of setting goals and working hard to accomplish those goals.

Thank you to my loving husband, John, for all his support and encouragement. Thank you for helping me turn my creative ideas into reality.

—*Kathy Young*

Table of Contents

Dedications ix

Introduction xv

1   Struggling to Learn 1

2   Losing Hope 5

3   Realizing Talents 9

4   Developing Job Skills 11

5   Gaining Self-Confidence 17

6   Buying My Own McDonald's Restaurant 21

7   Revealing My Secret 27

8   Helping Others Understand 31

9   Honesty Leads to Inspiration 39

Epilogue 41

Accolades for Eileen 45

This Story is True 46

Eileen's Secrets to Success 47

About the Author 48

Introduction

The Turning Point:
1994

"Welcome to McDonald's. Our Value Meal for lunch includes a hamburger, fries, and a drink. May I please take your order?" I asked as I stood by the cash register at the drive-thru window of one of the restaurants I owned. One of my employees told me that someone was on the phone waiting to speak to me. I was astonished by what I heard when I answered the phone.

"Hi, are you the owner?" asked the young and nervous voice on the other end.

"Yes, I'm Mrs. Kushner."

"Hi. My name is Jason and I'm in fifth grade. My class just read about you in the newspaper.."

"Oh, thanks for letting me know," I replied, shocked that anyone would care enough to call me.

"We read that you own restaurants near our school."

"Yes, I own two of them."

"We also read that you help lots of needy people."

"Yes, I try to help others."

"I have a learning disability just like you. I have trouble with reading, too," he said apprehensively.

My eyes welled up with tears as memories of my childhood flashed through my mind. I was the 49-year-old owner-operator of two McDonald's restaurants, but I had kept my own learning difficulties a secret for most of my life. Memories of how I struggled in school and at work were painful. Remembering how I felt when I was young made it hard for me to believe that an 11-year-old boy felt good enough about himself to speak openly about his learning disability. At 49, I still could not speak openly about my own learning disability.

"Oh, I see," was all that came out of my mouth.

"The kids in my class all have learning differences, too. We want to know if you could come to our school. Can you come and talk to us about how you became successful?" he asked with excitement mounting in his voice.

"Uh … I've never done that before," I murmured as my stomach started turning.

"Well, we have been studying people who overcame their disabilities, and we want to meet you in person."

"I haven't talked a lot about my learning … disability, but I guess … if you really want me to do it … I suppose I could … ."

"Great! I'm glad that you're coming and I can't wait to tell the other kids in our class. I have got to go to my music class soon. My teacher, Mrs. Young, wants to talk to you to set up the date. Thanks a lot. Bye."

After I arranged the date with Mrs. Young, I sat there and reflected about what had just happened. Did I really commit to speaking in front of students? I wondered if I would *finally* be able tell these students about this part of my life that I had kept hidden for all these years.

Jason was in fifth grade when he met Mrs. Kushner

Eileen, Mom, Elliot, Dad, Steve

1

Struggling to Learn

My twin brother, Elliot, and I were born in 1944 in Fort Wayne, Indiana. We both suffered from learning disabilities, but we would not understand until mid-life why we did poorly in school during our early years.

In elementary school, reading was very hard for me. I read slowly, very slowly, and struggled to figure out the words. It helped me keep my place if I followed along with my finger underneath each word as I read.

"Eileen, it's your turn to read out loud," I heard my teacher say.

I immediately felt afraid, as I did every time I was called on to read. My hands began to sweat and they started shaking. My heart was pounding so hard that I thought people could hear it beating. With great effort, I quietly tried to sound out the words as I moved my finger across the page.

Suddenly, I felt a sharp sting across the back of my hand as my teacher hit it with a ruler.

"Stop using your finger to follow along," the teacher commanded. "Speak up so we can hear you!"

Reluctantly I continued, "Form ... *from* that day on the ch-ild ... child-ren ... *children* hopped ... *hoped* that the king w-wo-*would* ... ."

In the background, I could hear the other students laughing and whispering because they thought I was reading so poorly. I could see them rolling their eyes in disgust because I couldn't read as smoothly or quickly as they could. I was so embarrassed and that made it even harder for me to concentrate on what I was reading. It felt like everyone in the room thought that I was just "stupid."

"Eileen, are you really *trying*? You're reading so slowly that we can't understand what you're saying. We can't wait for you any longer," the teacher declared. "You need to start working harder." She glanced at me with a look of failure and called on one of the "smart" kids to pick up where I had left off.

My eyes burned with tears. I *was* trying. I wanted to read quickly like the other kids. I wished that I could be in the highest reading group and read harder books, but I couldn't. I wanted to enjoy writing stories like the other kids, but I had such a hard time getting my ideas from my brain onto the paper. When the teacher handed back their papers, they only had a few things to correct. When my written work was returned, there were countless words circled in red ink because they were misspelled. There were numerous mistakes with my grammar and punctuation. There were so many errors in my writing that it made it hard for anyone to understand what I was trying to communicate.

One teacher called me up to her desk. "Eileen, you're so lazy. You never take the time to spell all these words correctly. You forgot to put in punctuation," she added in a scornful tone. "This is not the quality of writing that I expect in this class. Your work is unacceptable, and you'll need to fix all your mistakes for homework."

"Okay," I mumbled. My head pounded. I took the paper, which seemed to be completely covered in red marks. My eyes filled with tears as I slowly trudged back to my desk.

Math was also a struggle for me. Story problems were hard to solve since I had trouble reading the words. And even though I practiced my math skills every night, I just didn't understand how to get the answer. I couldn't memorize all the math facts. I had to use my fingers, and it seemed like I didn't have enough of them to solve the problems. Counting money and making change were almost impossible.

In the third and fourth grades, I would raise my hand to ask for help with math all the time. My teachers grew impatient with all my questions, and the other students would shake their heads with contempt.

"I am passing out your assignment for today. Since it is Friday, we will be taking a review test. It will be easy since we have been working on these skills all week."

As I looked at the paper, my heart sank. I did not understand what I was supposed to do. I raised my hand to ask a question when I heard a boy behind me say, "She's so dumb. She never gets it. The teacher has already explained everything twice."

The teacher walked over to me and asked "Weren't you listening? The rest of the class has already started working. Stop wasting our time and get started."

The kids belittled me because I kept requesting help, so I eventually stopped asking questions and sat in class feeling helpless and confused.

At home, my twin brother, Elliot, and I shared a special bond since both of us had learning disabilities. Other students teased both of us, but Elliot was more thick-skinned and ignored the insults. We were in the same homeroom classes through sixth grade. I called Elliot my "guardian angel" because he was always patient with me and gave me support whenever I needed it.

During class, I tried to sit behind him so I could hide from the teacher and not get chosen to answer questions. As soon as the teacher started asking students to read out loud, I would squirm, sliding down in my seat so the teacher couldn't see me. When kids picked on me, Elliot defended me. And, because he didn't want to seem smarter than his sister, there were many times that he would purposely make mistakes on exams. That way, both of us would get the same low grades.

Our father worked patiently with us to help us complete our school assignments. Each night, he would sit with us at the kitchen table. He would go over and over and over our spelling words. He would pronounce each word again and again, trying to help us learn how to spell even the simplest words.

"Eileen, the next word that you need to spell is *middle*," my father stated.

"Ummm, let's see," I stammered. Slowly, I whispered, *"M-i-d-e-l?"* phrasing my attempt as a question.

"No, try again," my father said. He sounded angry to me at the time, though I realize now that he was frustrated because he did not know how to help us.

"Is it *m-i-d-d-e-l?*"

"Eileen, we had this word yesterday. You need to remember that the word is spelled *m-i-d-d-l-e*. We will keep working on these words until you can spell them correctly," sighed my father, who worked long hours six days a week and still made time to help us with our homework.

As our father spelled a word out loud, Elliot would scribble it on a piece of paper. The paper was hidden below the table, out of our father's sight. Only Elliot and I could see the paper. We would look at it when we were asked to spell the words out loud. We both felt guilty about this, as if we were cheating, but it was the only way we could spell some words correctly. Both of us loved our father, and we did not want to disappoint him.

Our older brother, Steve, did not have learning difficulties. Schoolwork was a breeze for him. As Elliot and I were working with our dad in the kitchen, Steve would usually be sitting in the other room. He was happily doing crossword puzzles, since all his schoolwork was finished.

"Steve, I can't believe you're actually having fun doing those," I told him.

"Are you kidding? Crossword puzzles are simple!" he said with a smile.

"It doesn't make sense to me that you could enjoy doing that. How do you remember how to spell all those words?"

"I think spelling is *so* easy," Steve replied.

I was amazed. To think that anyone would like to play Scrabble or other word games! For me, anything involving words was painful. It was as bad as having a cavity filled at the dentist's office.

2

Losing Hope

When I was nine years old, I became ill with a kidney disease. My parents were told that the chances I would survive were not good. I was in the hospital for quite a while before they found medicine that helped me. For almost two months, I was too weak to walk, and I missed three months of school. Even though Elliot brought home my assignments during my absence, I slipped farther and farther behind.

When I was 11 years old, my sixth grade teacher told my parents, "Don't expect anything from Eileen. Your daughter is lazy and will never amount to anything."

At the end of sixth grade, both Elliot and I received failing grades. It was decided that both of us would repeat that grade. But this time, Elliot and I would be placed in different classrooms.

When my mother told me the news, I started trembling uncontrollably and sobbing that I would never make it without my brother. I was terrified because I counted on his support. Having him with me in the same class meant that there would be at least one person in the room who would not laugh at my mistakes. If I did get embarrassed, he had been there to give me a reassuring look or a say few words that let me know he was on my side.

"Eileen, things will be okay," said my mother trying to calm me.

Looking up at her with tears in my eyes I whispered, "I'm afraid of what will happen when Elliot isn't with me."

My mom hugged me and said, "You can't give up. We believe in you."

Eileen at age 9,
months after she came
home from the hospital

My second attempt at sixth grade was difficult for me. Students and teachers continued to make me feel bad about my skills in reading, spelling and math. Even though Elliot wasn't in my class, he continued to watch out for me. Since our classrooms were next door to each other and we had the same bell schedule, we would see each other in the hall frequently. He would always check with me to see how things were going and try to make me feel better. Each day he sat with me at lunch.

My parents and Steve continued to assist me with my assignments. It gave me strength to know that my family loved and valued me.

In seventh grade, I tried out for the cheerleading squad. I didn't make the regular squad but was chosen to be an alternate. This meant I could cheer if one of the girls on the squad had to miss a game. If any of the girls left the squad, I would be her replacement.

My dream came true when one of the girls on the squad quit right before the first game. I was thrilled! I would finally be a member of a team. My classmates would look up to me now. My family could be proud of me now. They were so eager to watch me cheering with the girls in the first game of the season. As my parents took photographs of me, I felt so important. I was wearing the cheerleading uniform, a white v-neck sweater with red and white trim. I wore a red skirt, white bobby socks and gym shoes, and proudly held my red and white pom-poms.

The game was held on a Friday. It was the same day that report cards came out. As soon as the game was over, the cheerleading coach marched up to me and shoved a card in my face.

"Look at these grades! Eileen, we have strict rules," she said angrily.

I tried to focus and realized that she was holding my report card. I was amazed that she had gotten my grades so quickly.

"Cheerleaders have to get good grades, and your report card has C's and D's. We can't have you on the squad with these grades. You'll have to turn in your pom-poms and your cheerleading sweater. If you want to be a cheerleader, you have to try harder in school."

It shocked me to realize that the cheerleading coach felt that I had not been trying. I had been working as hard as I could to get those "terrible" grades. I had spent hours and hours working on homework. I did not know how I could have worked any harder.

As I turned in my uniform, I could hear the other cheerleaders snickering. The girls kept asking me why I was turning in my sweater. I felt humiliated and embarrassed. I finally whispered, "I had bad grades."

Choking back the tears, I ran from the locker room. For such a long time I had imagined what it would be like to be on the cheerleading squad. Wearing that uniform, I had felt on top of the world. Being a cheerleader had been my chance to show everyone that I had a talent. Now, again, I felt like a failure.

It was wintertime, and the temperature was frigid at night. I began to sleep with the window open, hoping I would get really sick. Each night I prayed that I would die so no one would ever bully me again.

At the age of 11 her parents were told, "Your daughter will not amount to anything."

3

Realizing Talents

I didn't fall victim to the freezing cold of my bedroom, and as time passed, my life did improve—but only because my family continued to support and encourage me. It always comforted me to know that my family loved me.

While I was in high school, I had many successes, although none of them were academic. While my grades in Math, English, Social Studies and Science remained low, I earned A's in Art, Music, and Physical Education (P.E.), places I could thrive without having to take tests or complete reading assignments.

In fact, I outperformed most of the girls in my P.E. classes. I was the second fastest runner in the whole school. My athletic abilities made me a favorite of the P.E. teachers. If they had a new skill to teach, they would call on me to demonstrate it to the rest of the class. Teachers also told me that I was a great singer, so I auditioned and was accepted to join three different choruses. It was thrilling to try out for something and make it! Since it was hard for me to read the musical notes, I memorized all the music. Art was easy for me because I was creative, and loved hands-on projects. Students were impressed by my abilities in Art, Music and P.E. and would ask me for help in those subjects.

During high school, I gained confidence. My successes in nonacademic subjects made me feel more comfortable with myself. I was friendly and well-liked by others. Everyone enjoyed my sense of humor. For the first time in my life I loved coming to school since I was having fun and felt accepted.

Another reason why I enjoyed high school is because that is when I met my future husband. The first time I spoke to Larry, I was at a party when I was 15 years old. At that time, I was going out with his best friend. A year later, Larry met me again at another party and finally asked me out on a date. I accepted and we began a relationship that has lasted over 50 years.

Both Elliot and I loved our Senior year in high school. Since I had earned enough credits in my academic courses, I only took nonacademic classes. My grades were terrific! My name was even printed in the newspaper because I was on the honor roll. Elliot's academic skills had improved, and he was doing well in his classes, too. He decided that he wanted to get a college education.

Both of us graduated from high school. Elliot went to Michigan State University, and I married Larry when I was 18 years old.

High School Graduation

4

Developing Job Skills

Larry and I moved to Oak Park, Michigan. I felt that being a stay-at-home mom was the only choice I had for a career. I excelled at being a wife to my husband, Larry. He worked full-time at a bank, had a part-time job and took college classes at night. I was a devoted mother to our three girls—Laura, Debbie and Elyse. Cooking, cleaning, organizing, volunteering and parenting brought me great joy.

I spent countless hours helping my daughters with their schoolwork. At this time, I was still unaware that I had learning disabilities, so I didn't assume that any of my children had learning issues. I wanted to make sure that my children would not struggle in school the way I had, so I reviewed skills with them patiently. Since I was creative, I tried to teach them in ways that were more hands-on and fun.

Even though I could not pronounce or read most of the words on my daughters' weekly spelling lists, I practiced with them until they memorized their words.

"Okay, Elyse, I think the first word on your list is *o-rig-in-al*."

"Mom, I think you mean *original*. The teacher said that if someone invents something new, then it's *original*."

"Oh, yeah. Sure, of course, the word is *original*. Can you spell that for me, please?"

I used a pencil to keep track of each letter as Elyse spelled it out loud and then I said, "Perfect. Tell me the word again, and then I want you to use the colored chalk to write that word on this small chalkboard." My efforts with my girls paid off, and they usually got A's on their spelling tests each week.

When I read aloud, I still struggled and would skip words or make up words as I went along. I wanted to spend time reading with my girls, and I figured out that *Go Dog Go*, written by Dr. Seuss, was the only book that I could read aloud to my girls without stumbling on any of the words. Each night, I loved to snuggle and cuddle up with them as I read that same book over and over again. The time we spent reading together was a gift that I gave to them and to myself. It gave me a sense of accomplishment and made me feel like I had won the lottery.

By the time all of my children were enrolled in school, I was 31 years old. Being a wife and mother had made me feel safe because I could wake up each morning without worrying about how I would make it through the day. No one was belittling me. I never received a bad report card about my skills as a wife and mother. The report cards that I did see were the ones that my girls brought home, and they were getting excellent grades. However, at this point I desperately needed to get a job to help support our family.

One day, I looked in the refrigerator and cabinets and realized that we had no milk or bread or fresh food to feed the girls. Neither Larry or I had any money left in our bank accounts. We had never applied for charge cards. We waited until the end of that day when Larry brought home his paycheck to go shopping for food. Larry was ready to drop out of college to get another part-time job. He missed spending time with the girls, but I encouraged him to continue to work toward his dream of getting a college education.

The thought of working outside the home made me feel uncomfortable. I had no self-confidence and knew that any job would require skills in reading, math or writing. In those days, there were no computers or calculators. I thought about what job I might be good at and came up with the idea to work at the local floral shop since I am so good with my hands. It took every ounce of courage I had to talk to the owner of the nearest shop.

I washed and ironed my blouse and skirt that I had purchased at K-Mart, shined my shoes, polished my nails, did my hair and put on my make-up. I looked in the mirror and said to myself, "Why wouldn't he hire me? It won't be difficult for me to cut flowers and arrange them in vases."

Before I opened up the door to the flower shop, I took a deep breath and kept telling myself that this would work out.

I entered the shop and a middle-aged gray haired man said, " Can I help you purchase some flowers?"

"I'm not here to buy flowers, but I'd like an application to work here."

"Why do you want to work at my shop? Why would I want to hire you?" Mr. Ross, the owner, growled as he kept working on an arrangement.

"I'll work hard every day, and I'll never be late," I pleaded, "I'll give you a hundred and fifty percent. In fact, you don't have to pay me right away. Let me volunteer for a while, so I can prove to you that I can do the job." In my mind, I felt that I was not good enough to get paid. I just wanted a chance.

"Do you have any experience? Have you ever worked with plants and flowers?"

"No, but I would like to learn," I said, my voice dropping.

"I don't have time to teach you," he snarled at me. "You have no experience. You don't have any skills. I don't need you, and I don't want you working here."

Feeling rejected and depressed, I quickly walked out the door telling myself that I would never be able to get a job since I couldn't do things as well as other people. I pictured a balloon in my mind and that man had just poked a pin into it so that all the air escaped.

When I got home, I told Larry what had happened. Larry thought about his friend, who was a manager at a McDonald's restaurant. He said he would ask his friend if I could work for him.

A few days later, I went for the interview even though I thought it would be a waste of time. I put on my same outfit and prepared myself for another humiliating experience. I couldn't let Larry down.

At 10:00 on a Tuesday morning I walked into the McDonald's restaurant and asked one of the crew people if I could talk to Carl since he was expecting me.

A few minutes later, a young blond-haired man wearing a white shirt with a blue tie walked over to me and shook my hand. He looked me straight in the eyes and said, "Eileen, I hear that you are looking for a part time job at my McDonald's. Larry told me that you can only work from 10:00 a.m. to 2:00 p.m. since you have your three children coming home from school at 3:00. At McDonald's, we have shifts to accommodate everyone's needs."

"I think that Larry told you that I have never worked at a restaurant before, right?" I asked.

"At McDonald's, we have a great training program, and we'll get you up to speed in no time."

Carl took me on a quick tour of the restaurant and gave me a brief explanation of the various stations: french fries, milk shakes, grill, lobby and the cash register.

"Well, Eileen, would you like to start working here on Monday morning at 10:00? We will teach you how to put the ice cream in the cup, add the syrup and then mix it to create our delicious milkshakes. After you have mastered the milkshake station, we'll teach you how to cook and bag the fries. How does that sound to you?"

I looked at Carl in disbelief. *Was he really offering me a job at McDonald's?* I thought.

"Carl, does this mean that you want me to work here?"

"Yes, I'm sure that you will fit right into our McDonald's family."

"Oh my gosh, I'm so excited. I know that I'll be able to make the shakes and fries. Thank you. Thank you so much."

"When you come on Monday I'll give you your own blue polyester shirt and pants, a hat and a name tag. You will be all set. Do you have any questions?"

"Larry will be so thrilled. I'll see you on Monday."

As I drove home, I felt many emotions: anxious, nervous, worried, pleased and hopeful.

After I had worked at that McDonald's for six months, Carl approached me. He said, "You are such an excellent worker that I'm going to promote you. You'll work at the cash register taking orders. You'll add up the cost of the items and handle the money."

"You promised that I would only make fries and shakes," I begged.

"Yes, but I've seen how hard you work. I've seen how well you get along with everyone. I would like you to work at the cash register so you can interact with the customers. As they give you their order, all you need to do is write down the prices on this pad of paper. Then add all the numbers to find the total. The customer will pay you, and then you'll figure out how much change to give back. I'm sure that you won't have any trouble. It's so easy."

I panicked as I remembered trying to make change in my classes at school. The kids laughed at my mistakes.

Larry didn't understand that I had any difficulty with reading or math. When I went home that day, as soon as I saw Larry, I started sobbing like a baby and could hardly catch my breath. Finally, I composed myself enough to say, "I have to quit my job."

"Are you kidding? Why do you have to quit?" he asked, looking at me with a puzzled expression his face.

"The manager wants me to work at the register. I can't do that job. I can't make change. I can't work there anymore."

Seeing how upset I was, Larry gently hugged me. "I'll teach you how to do it."

Through my tears, I sniveled, "Really, are you sure you can teach me?"

"Of course, Eileen. I work at a bank, so I know how to train people to count money. It's no big deal. You won't have to quit."

I went to work the next day and asked Carl if I could bring home receipt pads, sheets with menu prices, empty hamburger boxes, French fry bags, and cups. He asked me why I needed those things, so I told him that I wanted to practice at home so I could be ready to be trained for the new position. He seemed surprised, but he was busy and didn't question me. Each night, Larry and I sat at the kitchen table and practiced. There were no computers at McDonald's then, so I had to write down the prices and add up the totals. Larry would give me more money than the total amount so I would have to make change. We practiced like this every night until I gained confidence.

I took the job promotion. Eventually, I trained other employees to work at the cash register.

McDonald's SYSTEM			
178015			
MAY I HAVE YOUR ORDER PLEASE? MAY I HELP YOU M'AM (SIR)?			
HAMBURGERS	.15 ea.		
McDouble Hamburgers	.28 ea.		
CHEESEBURGERS	.20 ea.		
McDouble Cheeseburgers	.38 ea.		
FISH SANDWICH	.24 ea.		
FRENCH FRIES	.15 ea.		
MILK-SHAKES ☐ Chocolate ☐ Strawberry ☐ Vanilla	.22 ea.		
COKE Extra Large	.10 ea. .15 ea.		
ORANGE Extra Large	.10 ea. .15 ea.		
ROOT BEER Extra Large	.10 ea. .15 ea.		
MILK	.12 ea.		
COFFEE ☐ Cream	.10 ea.		
HOT CHOCOLATE	.12 ea.		
Sub Total			
Sales Tax			
TOTAL			
McDonald's Corporation Trademark Reg. U. S. Pat. Office			

Employees used this form to calculate the total amount

5

Gaining Self-Confidence

Five years after I started working at McDonald's, Carl transferred to a different McDonald's. Things were good with the new manager, Lou. He often complimented me on the respect that the other employees showed me and the competent job that I was doing. Unfortunately, Lou changed after he started having personal problems. One day I went to work and Lou was sitting with the owner of the McDonald's in the office. He called me over and told me that I wasn't needed at his store any more. When I asked why, he never gave me a specific reason. I was just told that I was fired. I was heartbroken because I felt it was truly unfair. How could this happen to me?

Since I needed to earn money for my family, I registered at the local unemployment office. The clerk asked me a few questions and then gave me lots of forms that I needed to complete. As I turned to leave, I looked around and could see dozens and dozens of dejected unemployed people standing there clutching those same humiliating forms in their hands. At that moment, I decided that I was never going to collect an unemployment check since there was nothing wrong with me. I just needed to look for a different job. Lou might have broken my spirit, but I was not going to let him break me.

Larry tried to be helpful and found me a job as a secretary. There was one small problem and it was that I couldn't spell, write letters or file alphabetically—so I was fired from the job after only two weeks.

When Larry heard the news, he consoled me and said, "Don't dwell on your weaknesses. Dwell on your strengths. You just need to find a job to match your abilities."

Still uncertain about my job skills, I went to a vocational center. There, I took some tests to see what types of jobs would suit my skills.

A psychologist prepared to share the test results with me. As I tried to focus on his words, my hands trembled. I felt sharp pains in my stomach. Tears filled my eyes as I remembered when my teachers told my parents that I was a failure. I remembered how ashamed I had felt. I took a deep breath since I expected to feel humiliated again. But, to my surprise, the words that came out of the psychologist's mouth were not, "You're a failure."

"Eileen, the tests showed that you are very intelligent. You have strengths in many areas."

Who he is talking about? Me? Can this be true? I nearly looked over my shoulder assuming he must be speaking to someone else.

I was overwhelmed! It was unbelievable that a test could actually prove that I was smart. What about all those bad grades I'd gotten in school?

The man then went on to say, "You have learning disabilities in reading, spelling and math. That makes it hard for you to learn."

I looked at him and really didn't understand what he was saying. "Learning disabilities" was a brand new term in my vocabulary.

"What does that mean?"

"A learning disability affects the brain's ability to receive, process, store or respond to information. People with learning disabilities have average or higher intelligence and may have difficulty with reading, spelling, math, writing or reasoning. It is a lifelong challenge but, with support and intervention, people with learning disabilities can succeed."

"I wish I'd known about this a long time ago, but I'm relieved that I know now."

"Eileen, when you were in school in the 50s and 60s, there were no programs in public schools to help children with learning disabilities. In the 1970s, laws were passed that required schools to provide special education services for students who have learning disabilities."

Finally, I knew that there was a reason why learning was so hard for me. My parents' faces appeared in my mind, and I wished that they were still alive so they could have shared this wonderful moment with me. Then the psychologist told me about other bright and creative people with learning disabilities. The list included Leonardo Da Vinci, Picasso, Thomas Edison, Henry Ford, Alexander Graham Bell, Louis Pasteur, Nelson Rockefeller, Winston Churchill, Woodrow Wilson, Mozart, Beethoven, General George Patton, George Burns and Hans Christian Anderson.

It took my breath away to discover that all these smart people had trouble learning *just like me!* What a turning point in my life!

After a few days, the psychologist met with me again. He suggested that I work with him to gain confidence. I met with him for individual sessions and, later, with a small group.

The psychologist felt that because I didn't believe in myself, I was giving up too easily. He asked me to wear a rubber band on my wrist and told me to snap it each time I said the word "can't." He told me that this would help teach me not to use that word, but I was skeptical and did not believe a rubber band could change my thinking.

For over a year, I snapped that rubber band many times until my wrist became red and swollen. My whole family tried to help me, and they would keep encouraging me to not use the word "can't." It was emotionally and physically difficult, but, eventually, I stopped using the word. Amazingly, this process helped me to focus on what I *could* do.

The other daily homework assignment given to me by the psychologist was to look at myself in a mirror and repeat 10 times, "I like myself, and I'm okay." At first, I could only say it while I looked down at my feet. Every week he reminded me that I needed to stare at my eyes in the mirror. The goal was that I would learn to like myself for who I was in spite of my disabilities. For many months, I felt this was the hardest thing I had to do each day. But I kept working at it for almost two years until I was finally able to say those words and believe them.

Finally, I knew that I had learning disabilities. But I did not understand much about what that meant—only that my struggling all my life now made sense. Still, I was scared to share the "label" with others since I was apprehensive about how people would react.

6

Buying My Own McDonald's Restaurant

Larry and I were struggling financially, so I had to find work again. With Larry's encouragement, I called the McDonald's Corporation. They told me there was a job opening at a McDonald's restaurant near our home. I worked at this store for a few years, and then I went to work at a different McDonald's. Working at different stores taught me a great deal about running a restaurant. I was getting good at it, and I was gaining confidence in my own abilities. One owner planned to move to Florida and open up four restaurants. He asked me if I wanted to move my family and manage all of his new stores.

But I had made a huge decision. "I don't want to move," I told him. "I want to own my own McDonald's." Before long, Larry and I were filling out applications and sending them to McDonald's Corporation.

That year, over 10,000 applications were sent to the corporate office for the rights to own a restaurant. McDonald's chose only 1,000 applicants to interview. I was one of them.

When I arrived at the corporate office in Southfield, Michigan, an image flashed in my mind of the housewife and mother who felt that she had no job skills. I also saw the image of a confident woman who had the skills and abilities to become an owner-operator of a McDonald's.

I met with three well-manicured and professionally dressed McDonald's executives. After introductions were made, we spent a little time just getting to know each other. I thanked them for inviting me to come and, before I could stop myself, I blurted out, "Why do you want to interview me?"

The man replied, "We have seen how you interact with your customers and employees. You always make sure to do whatever needs to be done, even if it means working harder or longer than others. We like that. We don't want to choose someone who can easily afford to buy a restaurant and just write a check. We want people who will work hard to run a successful business. We believe you are one of those people."

I went through two interviews with McDonald's executives. Then Larry came with me for a third interview. Of the 1,000 interviewees, only 100 would be chosen to own restaurants throughout the country that year.

For weeks, I waited to hear back, but I never gave up hope. Finally, I received a phone call that would change my life.

"Hello, Eileen. This is Mr. White from McDonald's Corporation," came the voice from the other end of the line. "Congratulations! We'd like you to be an owner-operator of a McDonald's restaurant."

"Oh, my gosh!" I screamed as I jumped up from my chair and almost dropped the phone. I started dancing around the kitchen and accidently stepped on the dog. "Wow! This is unbelievable! Thank you so much. I'm thrilled!"

"You'll have to go to school to learn how to own a restaurant," Mr. White told me. "We'll send you to Hamburger University in Oak Brook, Illinois. You'll take classes for two weeks and will need to pass the required tests."

I took a deep breath. Tests? Would I be able to pass them? *How would I be able to fake it? I'd never done well in school. How could I possibly make it through Hamburger University? How could I pass the required tests without anyone finding out about my learning disability?*

My mind flashed back to looking at myself in the mirror, standing there with my head high, repeating over and over again, "I like myself, and I'm okay." I looked down at my wrists and recalled the sting of the rubber band. Something changed in me. Suddenly, I *believed* that I could do it!

Two hundred people were in my class at Hamburger University. Each day, we were taught new concepts, and we were given a test at the end of each class. Test scores were posted next to each person's Social Security number the following day. Every morning, I would look for my score. And every morning, I would see it at the very bottom of the list. I was there, and I was trying my hardest, but on paper, I was failing again.

When I returned home from my two-week learning experience, I received a phone call from Mr. Stone, an executive at McDonald's Corporation. He knew me and had seen me working at the other restaurants for many years.

"Eileen, what happened?" Mr. Stone asked. "Were you trying your best? You got the worst grades of all the students in your classes!"

"Forget about the test scores!" I demanded. "You know I can run a store. You've seen me work. I need a chance to prove what I can do."

Mr. Stone agreed with me that I had the ability to run a business, so he talked to the other executives in the McDonald's Corporation about my positive qualities. He told them how my efforts had improved sales. Mr. Stone told the corporate people to look beyond the test scores and focus on the success of the stores that I managed. He told them about my work ethic and recommended that I be given a chance to own a restaurant. Mr. Stone changed my life, and, because he believed in me and my ability, he was able to make other people believe in me, too.

After a week, Mr. Stone called to say that the McDonald's Corporation had decided to ignore my test performance because they knew that I was such a hard worker. They would give me the chance to buy a restaurant. The one they had in mind was in a Chicago suburb.

I greeted the news with mixed emotions. It was true that I wanted my own restaurant, but I hated the thought of leaving the area in Michigan that I had known for 30 years. For a time, I had thoughts about saying "no" and continuing to work as a manager. But the dream of owning a restaurant was staring back at me. I was not going to give up.

Larry and I had to sell our home. We borrowed money so we could afford the down payment on the restaurant. Once we had everything in place, Larry, our three kids, my 85-year-old aunt, a parakeet, a dog and I piled into a van. We drove to our new home in Illinois, which was near the town where my brother, Steve, lived with his family.

Larry got a job at a bank, while I worked at our new restaurant 80 to 90 hours each week. The restaurant was located an hour away from our home. At least six days a week I had to be there by 4:30 a.m. and stay until closing, so I hardly had any time to sleep.

I kept busy managing the crew, serving customers, ordering and organizing the supplies, cleaning bathrooms, scrubbing floors, wiping tables, counting money and doing whatever else needed to be done. There were many issues to deal with, including fixing broken equipment, hiring and firing crew people, retraining crew people, maintaining the landscaping and improving customer relations in the neighborhood. Thankfully, other McDonald's people helped me get through this tough period.

Being able to laugh at myself has always helped me get through some tense moments. After working many months with little sleep, I was in the back of my restaurant trying to move the hoses from an empty Coke tank to a full Coke tank. I was so tired that I reversed the hoses and instead of the Coke going into the drink system, it sprayed all over the whole storage room. The ceiling, wall, cups, lids, plates, plastic utensils, cardboard boxes and other equipment had thick, sticky, brown syrup splashed all over. It was a gooey mess! I could have cried but decided to laugh at my situation. When my employees saw what happened, they just pitched in and worked with me to clean everything. I've never made a mistake with the hoses since then.

My hard work paid off. After 19 months, I got another call from a McDonald's executive.

"Eileen, you're doing a wonderful job. We have a McDonald's restaurant that's for sale, and it's closer to your home. We'd like to let you take over that store. In fact, since we've seen how well you can run a business, we'd like to offer you the opportunity to own and operate *two* McDonald's restaurants that are near your home."

"I'll have to talk with my husband and my family. Thank you so much for believing in me." Tears of happiness filled my eyes.

Larry and I discussed the situation. Larry offered to give up his job at the bank so he could help me run both restaurants.

In bed that night, I remembered the day my teacher told my parents I would never amount to anything. And now I was the owner-operator of two McDonald's restaurants.

7

Revealing My Secret

1994

Owning two restaurants made me feel blessed since I knew not everyone had the opportunities I had experienced. I wanted to do whatever I could to help those who were less fortunate, so I donated lots of time and money to help schoolchildren, people with medical problems and low-income families. I developed training programs for mentally challenged and legally blind employees. I also established and ran The Book & Toy Mobile for children living in a government-subsidized housing complex near one of my stores.

Soon, I became well known as a caring community leader. McDonald's Corporation gave me the Ray Kroc Award for my community involvement. This award is only given to a few owners, so it was a tremendous honor to receive it. The Illinois Chamber of Commerce, the governor of Illinois, school districts and local towns recognized my contributions on behalf of needy children and families. Then one day, a newspaper reporter named Ruth called. She asked me if she could spend a few minutes interviewing me about my efforts to help others.

A week later, Ruth came to my house. She was easy to talk to, and I was comfortable with her in no time.

During the interview, Ruth asked, "Why are you so passionate about helping people?"

I gulped and said, "I do it because I have learning disabilities, and I don't want anyone to suffer the way that I did."

Suddenly, I realized that I had shared my secret and that it would be printed in a newspaper. My old insecurities came back, and I worried that if people read the truth about me, they would laugh.

After discussing my learning challenges, the reporter asked me about my strengths.

"I have great insight. I can find creative ways to solve problems. I can look at how things are done at McDonald's and see ways to simplify things. The corporation used a few of my suggestions about where to place equipment in new restaurants. Recipes that I adapted for vegetarian sandwiches and biscuits were used in many restaurants. My employees respect me because I am a hands-on owner. I work beside them doing everything that they have to do, whether it's emptying the trash or using the computerized cash register."

"That is all I need for now," said Ruth as she got up to leave. "Just so you know, I'm not exactly sure when the article will appear. Thank you very much for your time."

My assumption was that my interview would be written only as a short paragraph, and it would probably be buried deep in the pages of the newspaper. A few months after the interview, I was sitting in my pajamas eating breakfast when the phone rang.

"Eileen, did you see the Friday newspaper yet?" Larry shrieked.

"No, I'm working the late shift today, so I haven't had a chance to see it yet."

"Put on your shoes and go bring the paper inside. I'll wait for you to get it."

"Larry, what's the rush?"

"There's something you need to see in the Neighborhood section," he said with a smile in his voice.

I found some shoes, threw on a coat and ran to get the paper. When I looked at the front page of that section, there was a half-page story about me! There was also a large color photograph, showing me making French fries at our restaurant.

I gasped. It was unbelievable.

"Eileen, I'm so proud of you," Larry said to me over the phone. "Just think about how many people will read this article and learn about all your accomplishments. I'll stop at a store and buy more copies for the girls and for our friends in Michigan."

"Other people told me that they were going to write about me," I replied, "but Ruth is the first reporter who actually published an article about me. It's such a huge article! Do you think anyone will really notice it or take the time to read it?"

"Oh Eileen, of course, they'll read it. Your efforts have touched so many lives. Let's go out tonight and celebrate with a nice dinner."

"That sounds great. Thanks for letting me know about the article. You made my day!"

As I drove to the store, I felt nervous as I wondered what I would say to people if they had read the article. I shrugged my shoulders and told myself to stop worrying since no one would probably mention it to me.

When I walked into my restaurant that afternoon, I was totally shocked to see that my managers had hung copies of the article all over the windows and doors.

To my surprise, people treated me like a celebrity. For the next few days, customers made special trips to the restaurant just to thank me for educating the public about learning disabilities. Teachers, parents, grandparents and friends wanted to share their stories with me about their students or children who had learning difficulties. Adults with learning disabilities talked to me about their struggles. It was heartbreaking; so many of these people had tears in their eyes as they shared their experiences with me. Being open about my learning challenges changed the focus of my life.

This photo appeared in the first newspaper article written about Eileen. Jason and Mrs. Young called her after seeing this article.

8

Helping Others Understand

Jason and his Special Education teacher, Mrs. Kathy Young, had seen the newspaper article written by Ruth, and that was why he had invited me to speak. When I called Mrs. Young to set up the date for my visit to the school, I told her how impressed I was that Jason phoned and talked to me about his own learning disability.

Mrs. Young said, "I always take time to make sure that each student understands their learning disabilities and abilities. I also teach them strategies that will help them learn. Each year, we do my Learning Disabilities Simulation with 300 fifth graders. All the students get to experience what it's like to have difficulty reading, writing and processing information. They also experience what it feels like when someone is teased."

"I certainly know how that feels. I've never forgotten the mean things that kids said to me when I was in school," I confessed.

"We explain that students with special needs may get certain accommodations such as alternative materials, tests read orally, modified assignments or extra time and that it's fair because they learn differently," Kathy continued. "Our goal is to try to teach kids to be more accepting of students who have learning difficulties."

"It sounds like such a wonderful learning experience," I commented. "I hope that I can come to see it sometime."

"Yes, of course, we'd love to have you come. I'm sure that you could add great insight to the discussion we have at the end of the simulation. Now let's talk about your visit. My students are so excited that you're coming. Many of them have already prepared questions for you. In fact, one girl would like to interview you at a later date so she can write a report about you."

"She wants to do a report about me?"

"Yes, my students do research and write reports about famous people with learning disabilities. I think it would be great if we could include a report in our booklet about a successful person from our community. When you come to my class, Jason will give you a booklet filled with the reports that were written last year."

"I'm looking forward to meeting your students. Thanks again," I said as I hung up the phone. Immediately, I found some file cards and started jotting down ideas for my first speech. I had so much I wanted to share with the students.

Two weeks after Jason's phone call, I went to visit his school. On the bulletin board was a huge display of photographs of famous or successful people who have learning disabilities. These photos included artists, musicians, actors, government leaders, athletes, educators, scientists, authors, inventors and business leaders. It surprised me to see a laminated copy of the newspaper article about my life on display. It was humbling to realize that the story of my struggles and accomplishments was inspirational to students and adults.

A boy named Danny walked over to me as I stood by the bulletin board and said, "Did you know about all these people with learning disabilities?"

"No, I'm just fascinated. I had no idea that so many talented people had trouble learning."

"We wrote to some of them, and they sent us letters and autographed pictures. I wrote to a man who writes TV shows and lots of books even though he can't spell. He's really smart and has awesome ideas. After he types up his stories, his secretary fixes all of his spelling mistakes."

"I wish that I had a secretary when I was in school," I shared with Danny.

"When I was in elementary school I had a really hard time. I thought that the only job I could ever do would be as a garbage collector since I would never be able to graduate from college. Learning about these successful people has really boosted my confidence, and my new goal is to become an architect."

"I'm glad that you believe in yourself now. The sky is the limit."

Jason came to get me and then introduced me to his fifth grade classmates.

I said, "Thank you for inviting me to come. I'm proud to say that I own and operate two restaurants. I'm a loving wife, mother and grandmother. I'm organized and creative. I also have a learning disability. By telling my story, I hope that you will see that having learning difficulties doesn't prevent you from achieving success in life."

As I looked around the room, I noticed that the fifth grade special education students and their teachers were listening intently as I spoke. They didn't take their eyes off me as I moved around the room. As I shared my experiences, I could see that many of them could relate since they were gently nodding their heads in agreement. A few of the adults had tears in their eyes.

Before I left, one teacher came up to me and said, "Your speech really touched our hearts."

The speech that I gave to Jason's classmates was a turning point in my life. That visit made me realize that I needed to continue to tell my story to others. Mrs. Young was very involved in learning disabilities organizations, and she wrote proposals for both of us to speak at conferences. Our presentation explained how to develop self-awareness skills, self-advocacy and life skills in students. We traveled to four different states to make our presentations at schools and at state or international learning disabilities conferences. When I was a little girl, I never imagined that a room filled with teachers would listen to me speak. I never imagined that teachers would applaud my speech. I never imagined that teachers would come up to me after my speech and praise me. If only my parents were still alive to witness this accomplishment.

Both Mrs. Young and I were passionate about helping others. For over 14 years, her students would raise money to help needy children at local schools. They would make crafts to sell and posters to advertise our sale. Then they would sell candy and crafts at school and at my restaurant. We taught her students how to treat customers and how to make change.

The Social Worker from the local school gave us the names, ages and sizes of 50 or more needy children. After we raised the money, we took a field trip to Wal-Mart so Mrs. Young's students could shop for gloves, socks, clothes and small toys for each child. Finally, they wrapped and labeled hundreds of gifts.

When the principal from the local school came to pick up the huge bags of gifts, she told the students true stories of how these needy families lived. It was winter in Illinois, and these children desperately needed warm clothes. For example, she said that one family had four children and they had only one pair of gloves. Each child was allowed to wear the gloves one day each week. This annual service learning project helped Mrs. Young's students realize how fortunate they were and taught them the importance of giving back to the community.

Sharing my story taught me that many people didn't understand learning disabilities. I asked Mrs. Young if her students could create bulletin boards for my restaurants. The bulletin boards would teach customers about learning abilities and disabilities, and about learning strategies. For 16 years, a new class of fifth and sixth grade students would work together to make an educational bulletin board. Mrs. Young would hang it up at the restaurant and then her class would take a field trip to the McDonald's to see the display and meet me.

One December morning in 2009, about 20 students bounded off the bus and rushed into the restaurant to see their bulletin board. I shook hands with each of the excited students and asked them to show me their individual contribution to the project. The students proudly explained how they had developed the theme and done the research for their display. After they took seats in the dining area of the restaurant, I began my speech.

Eileen and Kathy
in front of their
educational boards

"Thank you so much for working on this wonderful bulletin board. Thousands of customers will see your creation throughout the year. Hopefully it will help them understand and accept people who learn differently, just like us. For most of my life, I tried to keep my learning difficulties a secret. It's so hard to keep others from finding out. Trust me, it was a relief when I discovered that I had a learning disability because then I knew I wasn't stupid, as I had been told in school. As I gained confidence in my abilities, I shared my secret. I found that people accepted me for who I am. In fact, I think people have more respect for me now that they know how hard I had to work to achieve my goals."

Maddy raised her hand and said, "When they told me that I had a learning disability, I was glad. I finally knew why learning to read was so hard for me. At first, I didn't want to be in the special education program. I was embarrassed about what the other kids would say about me. Well, I was put into a special reading class, and I started using materials that are different than the ones they use in my homeroom class. I've been learning phonics and practicing reading strategies, so my reading skills have really improved. Now I'm not worried about what the other kids think when I leave to go to Mrs. Young's class. I know the special reading program that we're using helps me. I just need to learn in a different way."

"I'm so glad that you're getting the help that you need," I said. "Reading is still hard for me, too, especially if I have to read out loud. In my religion, there are certain times during the holidays that I have to read passages out loud in front of many friends and family members. Even though I know my family won't laugh at me, I still get scared. I haven't forgotten how I felt when I read in front of the kids in school. My daughter has suggested that I just let someone else read for me, but I want to prove to myself that I *can* do it. Beforehand, I make sure that I read and practice the passage many, many times. If I practice, then I can read it out loud without stumbling. The key to success is to find strategies that work for you."

A student named Brad asked, "Are you the only one in your family who has learning disabilities?"

"Two of my daughters and one of my grandchildren have learning disabilities. My twin brother, Elliot, has learning disabilities and struggled in school just like me. During his senior year, his Physics teacher challenged him to do research, draw up a blueprint and create a perpetual motion machine. Elliot's machine was the best in the whole school. In fact, this invention helped him get accepted into college. He worked hard to complete degrees in Mathematics, Computer Science and Engineering, and he has written three books. Once he found his passion, he focused on it and achieved success."

Mrs. Young then motioned for a girl named Mari to come up to the front and stand by me since she had something she wanted to share.

Mari put a large clear plastic bag filled with seeds on the table and then she said, "Look at this bag of seeds. We're all like these sunflower seeds. We may not look as good on the outside or do things as quickly or do some things as well as others, but what is inside of us is what matters."

I smiled and added, "You're right. We're all smart on the inside. Those seeds have the potential to grow into beautiful flowers. The seeds may grow at different rates or may need to be watered or cared for differently. Each of you has the potential to grow into a successful adult. It may take some of you longer, or you may need to use different strategies or accommodations, but you all have the potential inside of you."

Suddenly I noticed a man carrying a professional camera. He and a woman holding a large pad of paper were waiting by the new bulletin board. The photographer and the newspaper reporter were there to take a photo for an article about the display that the students had created.

A few days later, there was a photo of the students and me on the front page of the newspaper. The headline read: *Local Role Model Inspires Others to Succeed*.

9

Honesty Leads to Inspiration

Many years after that life-changing phone call, Jason was in high school when he heard that Mrs. Young, her fifth grade students and I were doing a fund-raising event at one of my restaurants on a Saturday morning. We were raising money for a local man who needed a kidney transplant.

When I saw this confident young man walk towards me, I gasped with joy and excitement. "Jason! I'm so glad to see you again. Do you know that you're the one who taught me that I could help people if I told them about my learning difficulties?"

Jason smiled, hugged me and replied, "After all this time, I've never forgotten how you and Mrs. Young taught me that having Learning Disabilities means that I'm smart and just **L**earn **D**ifferently."

Throughout the restaurant, there were many colorful handmade posters advertising the fund-raising event. On a folding table, the fifth graders had arranged candy, crafts and their box for collecting the money. A woman had decided to make a purchase. She was fumbling in her purse, trying to find her wallet, when she remarked to a student named Adam, "I'm so impressed that you're giving up your Saturday to help others. What church or synagogue organized this project?"

"We're from a school near here. We have learning disabilities just like the owner of this restaurant," Adam responded.

The customer was surprised that an 11-year-old boy would be so open about his learning challenges.

But it all made sense when I introduced the customer to Jason and explained how his phone call, many years ago, had inspired me to finally share my secret.

Epilogue

Literacy
2010

by Kathy Young

*"Something almost magical happens when people break through obstacles
that hold them back and discover what is truly inside them."*
—Brad D. Diro

Each time that I heard Eileen tell her compelling life story, I watched the reaction of my students, their parents, and community members in the audience. Many of them had tears in their eyes. When she finished speaking, they rushed up to meet her as if she was famous. Seeing the impact this story had on hundreds of people over the years motivated me to record her story so students across the country would be able to read it. People who hear or read Eileen's story will gain a new understanding and acceptance of people with learning challenges.

Finding a publisher was truly formidable. I sent her story to John, a man with learning disabilities, who had published two books about literacy. We were shocked when he telephoned Eileen and told her that he wanted to arrange a conference call so that all three of us could talk.

"Eileen, I thought your book was wonderful, but your story is not finished," John stated.

"What do you mean?"

"The end of your story should be that you learned to read. You need to get tested and then find a tutor who will teach you how to read."

Tears were in her eyes as she said, "If they test me, I'm afraid that they will tell me that I'm stupid."

Both of us reminded her that the tests she took years ago showed that she was intelligent. We reassured her that these new tests would also prove that she was smart, and they would show why she had difficulty learning. The results would help a tutor understand how to improve her reading skills. We continued to encourage her and finally persuaded her to have an evaluation.

"Okay, John, I'll do it for you. I'll get tested so that Kathy will be able finish my story."

A few months later, Eileen was evaluated by a diagnostician named Sue. It was extremely difficult for Eileen to complete the tests, and she struggled for more than five hours. It was a stressful and emotional experience for her.

Eileen was terribly nervous when she met with Sue to discuss the results. Sue placed the diagnostic report in front of Eileen and said, "You're an amazing individual. Your inability to learn to read has nothing to do with your intelligence. The tests proved that you have severe limitations in your ability to process and remember sounds and letter patterns of the English language. You have a severe reading disability with classic symptoms of dyslexia. Your genetic makeup and neurological wiring has impaired your ability to learn to read, *not* your intelligence."

"If I'm smart, then why didn't I learn to read and spell?" she questioned.

"You weren't given the proper instruction. In order for you to learn to read, you need phonemic awareness and systematic, explicit phonics instruction. If you share the results of this evaluation with a specially trained tutor, she will know what methods or materials will help you learn the skills that you need."

"I'm too old," Eileen protested.

"It's never too late to learn to read," encouraged Sue. "John said that your story would only be complete if you learn to read."

"I'm too busy," replied Eileen. "I don't have the time."

"You've worked hard throughout your whole life, and I'm sure that you can figure out how to find the time. Your husband, family and workers will all support you. Here is a list of trained tutors. Please give one of them a call."

Eileen put the list of tutors in the file folder with her diagnostic report and put it in a drawer. A week later, she found the file and tried to read her report. It was frustrating because she struggled to decode most of the words. One section really caught her attention:

> The lack of decoding and fluency skills has nothing to do with your **intelligence**. The ability to process sounds and syllables is a very **teachable** skill. With intensive reading instruction, you could **learn to read**.

Intelligent — Teachable — Learn to read

It gave her hope to realize that if she was taught with the right methods, she could finally learn how to read. She was tired of struggling with her reading deficiencies and ready to take the steps necessary to become a reader.

Eileen took out the list of names of tutors and made a call that would provide the ending to her story.

Eileen began learning how to improve her reading skills when she was 65 years old!

Eileen was chosen to be on a
calendar of successful people

Accolades
for Eileen

- Presented her inspirational message at schools in numerous states, parent groups, colleges, community organizations and state/national special education conferences.

- Worked with Mrs. Young's students to raise thousands of dollars for needy families in the community.

- Received the Ray Kroc Award from the McDonald's Corporation for community involvement.

- Received awards from Illinois Chamber of Commerce for community involvement.

- Received an award from the Governor of Illinois.

- Received awards from numerous local school districts.

- Received awards from the cities of Buffalo Grove, Palatine and Arlington Heights in Illinois.

- Recognized as an extraordinary role model by The Omni Youth Services Society of LifeModels.

- Selected by the International Dyslexia Association to be on a calendar of Outstanding Dyslexics.

- Recognized for providing training programs for mentally challenged and legally blind employees.

- Recognized for establishing and running The Book & Toy Mobile for children living in government-subsidized housing.

- Scholarship established in her honor for high school seniors who plan to attend college.

This Story is True

Eileen Gold Kushner did keep her learning disability a secret.

Jason's phone call did change her life.

Jason is a computer technician.

Maddy is working as the Special Needs Coordinator at a school in Rwanda, Africa.

Danny is a lawyer.

Brad is a teacher.

Mari is a businesswoman.

Adam is a Television Production Manager.

Eileen and Kathy Young did develop a working relationship and lasting friendship based on their dedication to helping students who have learning disabilities.

Eileen's compassion to help others has made a difference in the lives of students, teachers, parents, customers and thousands of others.

Eileen and her husband have owned five different McDonald's restaurants.

Eileen and Kathy continue to travel throughout the country to educate teachers and parents about the importance of teaching students self-awareness skills, learning strategies and self-advocacy skills.

Self-awareness	(Understanding disabilities and using abilities)
Learning Strategies	(Understanding your own learning style)
Self-advocacy	(Knowing how to stand up for yourself)

Eileen's Secrets to Success

I feel that these life skills enabled me to become successful.

LIFE SKILLS	I encourage you to ...
INITIATIVE	Take action and get the job done.
PROBLEM-SOLVING	Figure out strategies to correct the problem.
PATIENCE	Take the time needed to do the job well.
FLEXIBILITY	Be willing to adapt to change.
CURIOSITY	Ask yourself "Why?" or "What if...?"
FRIENDSHIP	Be a loyal and considerate friend.
COMPASSION	Care about the needs of others, and help the less fortunate people in your community.
RESPONSIBILITY	Take the blame or credit for your actions.
ORGANIZATION	Create a system to keep organized and use it.
EFFORT	Keep working hard to accomplish your goals. You CAN do it!
PURSUE A PASSION	Discover and develop your talents.
PERSEVERANCE	Keep trying. Don't give up.
SELF-ACCEPTANCE	Believe in yourself and anything is possible.

About the Author

Kathy Young has dedicated her life to students with learning disabilities, as evidenced by numerous awards reflecting her teaching prowess and enthusiasm. She developed a series of L.D. Simulations that allow students and adults without learning difficulties to experience the learning process through the eyes of those who struggle. Her simulations have been used throughout the U.S. and Canada. She is also the author of the book *KidTips: Study Strategies for Students With Learning Differences.*

During her career in the public schools, Kathy taught students in third through sixth grade and in high school. She has taught graduate level classes in reading methods and made presentations at many state and national Special Education conferences. Since retirement, she has been working as a Curriculum Designer for an educational publishing company and writes materials to aid struggling readers. She volunteers at local schools so she can train teachers how to use her materials and continue to teach students.

Kathy and her husband, John, live in an octagon house that they largely built themselves with help from family members. They love traveling with their motorcycling friends to domestic and overseas destinations.

Kathy and John on one of their
motorcycling adventures

This is the poem that Jessica read at the assembly that was held when I retired. I dedicate this poem to the compassionate teachers who strive to make a difference in the lives of those students who learn differently.

—Kathy

If I Could Teach You, Teacher

If I could teach you, teacher,
I'd teach you how much more
you have accomplished
than you think you have.
I'd show you the seeds
you planted years ago
that are now coming into bloom.
I'd reveal to you the young minds
that have expanded under your care,
the hearts that are serving others
because they had you as a role model.
If I could teach you, teacher,
I'd show you the positive effect
you had on me
and my life.
Your homework is
to know your value to the world,
to acknowledge it, to believe it.
Thank you, teacher.

By Joanna Fuchs

Eileen's parents Etta and Dave Gold

Eileen and Larry on their wedding day 50 years ago

Eileen and her brothers Elliot and Steve

Eileen's daughters Deb, Elyse, and Laura

The whole family!

CPSIA information can be obtained at www.ICGtesting.com
Printed in the USA
LVOW110606230413

330457LV00001B/1/P